SIMON PETER
The Second Epistle

A Letter from Death Row

Gordon Kenworthy Reed

SIMON PETER
The Second Epistle

A LETTER FROM DEATH ROW
by Gordon Kenworthy Reed

Copyright © 2019 by Tanglewood Publishing

ISBN-13: 978-09972490-7-1

Unless otherwise indicated, Scripture quotations are taken from the ESV® Bible (The Holy Bible, English Standard Version®), copyright © 2001 by Crossway, a publishing ministry of Good News Publishers. Used by permission. All rights reserved.

Additional Scripture is taken from the New King James Version® (NKJV) (Copyright © 1982 by Thomas Nelson, Inc. Used by permission. All rights reserved.), The Living Bible (TLB) (Copyright © 1971. Used by permission of Tyndale House Publishers, Inc., Carol Stream, Illinois 60188. All rights reserved.), and the Christian Standard Bible® (CSB) (Copyright © 2017 by Holman Bible Publishers. Used by permission. Christian Standard Bible® and CSB® are federally registered trademarks of Holman Bible Publishers.)

All rights reserved. No part of this book may be reproduced in any form without written permission

Tanglewood Publishing
800-241-4016

Book Design and Layout by Capsicum Designs, Mieke Moller
Cover Design by Christy Rodriguez

Printed in the United States of America

DEDICATED TO THE MEMORY OF

Harold D. ("Rip") Baker
My "Jonathan"

Table of Contents

1. Abounding Grace 1
2. The Sure Way to Assurance 11
3. Holy Bible: God's Voice to Man.................................. 23
4. Holy Bible: Fact or Fable? 33
5. Holy Bible: More Than a Long and Rich Heritage.... 45
6. Danger: False Teachers Ahead 55
7. The Return of Christ: Good News/Bad News 67
8. The Return of Christ: The Scoffers 79
9. Motivation for Holy Living...89

1

ABOUNDING GRACE

2 Peter 1:1-11

Try to put yourself first in the shoes of Simon Peter, who wrote this letter, and then in the shoes of those who read it after Peter had been executed. Shortly before this letter was written, Nero had conspired with certain people to set fire to the city of Rome. When word began to leak out that the Emperor himself was in the back of this crime, he looked for someone on whom he could shift the blame. Since Christians were already hated, and since wild rumors were spreading about them, he announced that Christians had confessed to the fire, and the persecution began. Not just the leaders like Peter and Paul were arrested, but thousands of men, women, and children were killed in every conceivable way of cruelty. Some were burned as torches to light Nero's chariot races. Others were torn to pieces by wild animals in the arena, and some were crucified.

Peter was thrown in prison and expected a trial. He was probably convinced that he could prove that neither he nor any other Christian had anything to do with the fire. But this was not to be. Picture the scene. Peter in chains has just been told that Paul has been beheaded and that he, being a Jew, would be crucified the next day before the howling, jeering mob. What would become of the suffering, struggling church? There were even greater dangers than the terrible persecution through which they were going. Already, false teachers were corrupting the minds and the morals of many who professed to believe in Christ. In a few hours he would be dead, and so would many of the other leaders. Quickly, he requested a quill and some parchment. In God's providence, his last request was granted. Once before, he had written a letter to believers in a better time. But now he had but a few hours to tell believers things that would enable them to withstand the killing persecution and the more deadly inner corruption. Lovingly, he claimed the promise that Christ had made to him long ago that the Holy Spirit would speak through him and reveal Christ to the world. So put yourself in Peter's place. What will you say?

Now the execution has taken place. Peter and many other great and godly leaders are gone, and the Church is scattered. Somehow this letter was smuggled out of prison before Peter was taken to his cross to die. In secret, copies were made and circulated. You are a frightened believer in hiding and wondering about all that has happened and why. You have just been given a copy of the great Simon Peter's last will and testimony. This little scroll is the only thing standing between you and utter despair. You will treasure every line, every word. You will pray for understanding because you know the Holy Spirit has spoken through this apostle of Christ. You find a secret place and begin to read, even as unbidden tears pour down your face, almost blinding you.

> *Simon Peter, a bondservant and apostle of Jesus Christ. To those who have obtained like precious faith with us by the righteousness of our God and Savior Jesus Christ: Grace and peace be multiplied to you in knowledge of God and of Jesus our Lord, as His divine power has given to us all things that pertain to life and godliness, through the knowledge of Him who called us by glory and virtue, by which have been given to us exceedingly great and precious promises, that through these you may be partakers of the divine nature, having escaped the corruption that is in the world through lust. (NKJV)*

This doesn't sound like the lament of a condemned criminal, dying for a crime he never committed! This sounds like the words of a confident and victorious soldier of Christ; which are exactly what they were and still are.

Peter called himself both a slave and an

ambassador of a King far greater than Nero, and he reminded those who read this letter that they, too, have the same kind of faith he has, and that faith comes as a gift from our God and Savior Jesus Christ. This is a letter about saving grace. If you had time for only one quick note to your loved ones, or were permitted only a few minutes with them before you died, isn't this exactly what you would want to tell them; the story of God's grace?

I. Peter was a man who experienced saving grace.

Before the Lord came by the lake that day and called Peter to be His disciple, he really wasn't much but a big-talking, hard-cussing fisherman who thought he was really something. He was not educated or trained. He was not a paragon of virtue; but the Lord reached out to him, showed him His amazing power, and made him to become a fisher of men. When he challenged the Lord to allow him to walk on water, he gave into his fears, and only the hand of Christ kept him from drowning. He bragged about what a good Christian he was, ignored Christ's warning, and fell flat on his face when tested. Men gave up on Peter, but Jesus forgave him, restored him, and empowered him with the Holy Spirit. Grace, unmerited and unearned, had been his life story, so when he was facing death, what else did he have to talk about?

It was a gift, pure and simple, but it was a gift to be shared with others. Once Peter had been restored and filled with the Spirit, his whole life was focused on telling the old, old story that was so brand new and exciting. From this time on, Peter never thought about who was important in the Kingdom, never bragged about his courage or set himself above the simplest and weakest believer.

In fact, here we hear him putting himself in the same category with all redeemed sinners, and reminding them that they, too, shared a "like precious faith" with him.

Beloved, this is true greatness, true godliness: to recognize your brotherhood with all believers. Whenever you tend to think more highly of yourself compared to other believers, when you think you're too good or too knowledgeable to associate with some Christians, remember these words of this great man: "To those who have obtained like precious faith."

II. Peter knew that saving grace is neither alone nor static.

"Grace and peace be multiplied to you in the knowledge of God and of Jesus our Lord..." Once you have been given the precious gift of faith, by grace alone, that grace begins to multiply itself in your life and heart. You find God's grace covers all your sin, cleanses your heart and mind, and reaches out in loving concern to your fellow believers and to those who have never known God's great grace.

Peace is the natural consequence of grace. Once you know you are forgiven and accepted by God, that knowledge brings with it a profound sense of peace that grows and multiplies as you discover more and more of God's wonderful grace. In fact, the demonstration of peace in your heart and life is one of the most convincing testimonies to others.

Grace enables you to grow in your knowledge of God. The unbeliever says to God, "Prove to me your love and power and I will believe." God says to the unbeliever, "Believe and trust me and I will show you my love and power." When Peter talked about the knowledge of our God and Savior Jesus our Lord, he included the fact of faith; who Jesus is and what he has done for our salvation. Anyone who ever tells you that our Lord Jesus Christ is anything less than God, having always been God the Son from all eternity, is teaching you falsehood that is condemned by the Word of God. If your faith in Jesus Christ falls short of confessing Him as truly God with all the attributes and essence of the Father, that, Beloved, is not saving faith. But these great facts of faith must also become a personal experience in your life as they were in Peter's life.

III. The bright future for those who have experienced grace.

Isn't it absolutely amazing that a man who knew he was going to be cruelly executed the next day could talk about the future so optimistically? The modern psychologist would say Peter was in a state of denial. No, Peter had tried denial long ago and that almost destroyed him. Peter had received saving and living grace from the Lord Jesus, who also gave to him and us some exceeding great and precious promises, and by these promises we live and in them we die, knowing that whoever believes and lives in Him shall never die, not in the final sense. What promises were so powerful and real to a dying man that he could write this way? First consider that the One who made him these promises had calmed storms, healed the sick, cleansed lepers, raised the dead, fed five thousand men with a morsel, been transformed in Peter's presence into the glorified Son of God, and then had Himself risen from the dead. Peter had seen all that with his own eyes. Of course, he believed anything and everything Christ said, and so do I. And Jesus told him and us there is a heavenly home, and He will personally prepare and guarantee a place in that heaven for each and every one who believes in Him. Furthermore, He had promised that one day He would come again in power and glory to judge the world, and He would usher in an everlasting kingdom of righteousness and peace.

Because Peter believed these promises, his heart and life had been purified from the stranglehold of the world; and when on the next day he went to the cross, he would die in victory and confidence in that blessed hope in which he would participate. How about you? Where do you stand in all this? Could you talk like this to your loved ones and friends as you face death? Have you known the saving, transforming power of grace in your life? Can you confidently say, "When my eyes close for the last time on this earth, I will awake in the presence of my Lord?"

For Discussion and Reflection

1. In what ways have you witnessed the saving power of grace in your life?

2. How do you act upon these experiences of God's grace? How do you use them to maintain an awareness of the working of the Holy Spirit in your life?

3. "Grace and peace be multiplied to you in the knowledge of God and of Jesus our Lord" (2 Peter 1:2): How do you extend the gift of God's grace to those in your immediate circle of family, friends, and co-workers, as well as to strangers that you meet in the course of daily activities?

4. A culture of persecution and cruelty led to Peter's incarceration and execution. Considering his response to that culture, how do you respond to the aspects of our culture that defy the example that Jesus set for us?

5. If you found yourself on a "death row" of your own, would you have Peter's sense of victory and confidence in God's promises? Explore the reasons for your answer to this question.

2

THE SURE WAY TO ASSURANCE

2 Peter 1:1-11

Several years ago, I was visiting with one of the elders in the church I was serving at that time. He had been ill off and on over a period of many months and was in the hospital for a series of tests. The doctor who was taking care of him had just left before I arrived. I could tell Jim was very pensive and apprehensive about the outcome of these latest tests. His doctor had been very honest with him and had said, "Jim, I don't see any solution to your medical condition. There are so many complications, including your age, the serious wounds you received in combat in World War II, and the nature of this illness now. There are just not many things left to do that offer much hope for a cure." Jim shared all this with me, and the doctor's opinion came as no surprise to him or to me. As we talked and prayed together, he told me that for the first time in his life he understood how the people in prison, on death row awaiting execution, must feel. After all, his doctor had just told him he could not much longer survive the infection that was destroying his body. A few weeks later, he went to be with the Lord. I think he had known for a long time his end was drawing near, but the words of the doctor made it seem very real and very soon, which it was.

Simon Peter had just learned that he was condemned to die and had but a few hours to leave behind some last words for those he loved. By God's grace, and by the inspiration of the Holy Spirit, he wrote what we now call 2 Peter; the last of two letters from the chief of the apostles and one of the best friends of our Lord when He was on earth.

The first part of this letter was an appeal to believers to persevere and to grow in their relationship to Christ and their usefulness in the Kingdom. He offered three good reasons as motivation for this growing in grace, and a detailed plan on how to grow and mature in the faith.

I. The Reasons

 A. The Living Bible translates verse two this way: "Do you want more and more of God's kindness and peace? Then get to know Him better." Not a perfect translation perhaps, but the point is well made. God's grace is that saving power that protects us from hell, and at the same time changes our lives. The only possible way to ever have a deep and abiding peace is to understand grace, God's grace. So many Christians seem to think that they have to earn God's forgiveness by being good, and if they stop being good, God will stop loving them. Of course, God wants you to be good, as described in His word. But there is no possibility of anyone ever being good enough on their own to please God and earn salvation. The more you learn of God, the more you understand that it is by grace we are saved through faith alone.

B. On the other hand, we are warned in verses 8-9 that if we fail to grow and to develop a godly character, we are barren and unfruitful as far as serving God is concerned; as for ourselves, we are like blind people, groping and hoping, and stumbling from one failure and sin to another. Is that the story of your life? Is that what you want your life to be? Is that why Jesus suffered so much and died for you? Of course not! An unfruitful, spiritually blind Christian is a contradiction and furthermore has no experience of real inner peace and no reason for it.

C. The third reason for building on the foundation of grace and becoming a strong and effective believer is your own sense of assurance that you really are a true Christian and will be welcomed into God's heaven when you die. Peter put it this way, "...be all the more diligent to confirm your calling and election, for if you practice these qualities you will never fall. For in this way there will be richly provided for you an entrance into the eternal kingdom of our Lord and Savior Jesus Christ." God knows those whom He has elected in Christ, and God has saved them by His almighty grace, but how can YOU know if you are one of those upon whom God's grace rests? How can you know if you are truly saved? That question doesn't have to wait for Judgment Day to be answered. Peter gives us the answer right here in this letter from death row. He shows just how to build a strong inner life that brings with it assurance and great peace. These words were based on his own experience. Once, in the upper room, he had a false sense of security based on his own strength, but he lost that when a rooster crowed just before dawn. But the kind of assurance he had when he was awaiting death was far different. It was based on forgiveness and the work of the Holy Spirit in his life. He had been preparing for death by the way he lived, and his confidence was in Christ. Don't you want that kind of assurance and peace, to really know you are saved and on your way to heaven?

II. The Sure Way to Assurance

This formula or blueprint may be compared to the step by step building of a house or, better still, of a church. It is not only an architect's drawing of the finished product, but also the builder's working drawings of how to make the vision a reality. Or this plan could be a map of how to arrive at the desired location in a place called, "Assurance and Peace."

2. THE SURE WAY TO ASSURANCE

There is another way of describing this.

Several years ago, while we were still living in Sardinia, South Carolina, one of the ladies there asked Miriam to knit her a fancy wool cover for her teapot, known as a tea cozy. So in her usual thorough and methodical way, Miriam first sat down and sketched the plan and the color scheme, and then set to work. I watched her at times as she was working simultaneously with several different colors all at once and was amazed to see the intricate pattern taking shape. She couldn't work through one color and then to another; she had to work all together at the same time. When it was finished, it was truly a work of art. What Peter is doing here is taking several threads of truth and weaving them into a beautiful pattern of the Christian life. And that's how it is in the experience of the believer. You can't just work on one part of being a Christian and then go back and pick up the rest. You can't just be meek and humble, you have to be pure and forgiving, and hunger and thirst after righteousness all together and at the same time.

So here from the pen of a man about to die for Jesus' sake, the Holy Spirit shows us the kind of persons God wants us to be, and indeed must be, if our claim to faith has any validity, and if our faith gives us any joy, peace, and assurance.

A. The anchor point is FAITH. That is where the Christian life begins, but it never ends there, and though faith alone saves, faith that saves is never alone. Faith is always accompanied by other graces and, like faith, these, too, must be developed - diligently. Peter had just written that God has given us all we need for life and godliness, and then he added that we are to give all diligence to develop a full Christian character.

B. "Add to your faith VIRTUE." That means we must blend in virtue with faith, or knit the strand of virtue around the main thread of faith. The word 'virtue' has a broad range of meaning. It certainly means moral excellence or, simply put, goodness. But it may also mean courage or bravery in the face of danger. Don't be fearful of what the future may hold; God is in control. Don't fear death or eternity beyond because Christ has defeated death and awaits you in eternity. He is your Shepherd now and will be then.

C. KNOWLEDGE is not only an awareness of certain facts about God and salvation, but it is an inward confidence that what God reveals is true; tried, tested, and true. This knowledge speaks of an ever-deepening relationship with the Lord, and ever-growing confidence in His Word. Those who know the Lord in their hearts and are firmly grounded in His Word also have:

D. SELF-CONTROL and PERSEVERENCE. These two ideas go hand in hand and are entwined together and are added to faith and knowledge.

2. THE SURE WAY TO ASSURANCE

John J. Sullivan was one of the first and maybe the greatest heavy weight boxing champion of the world. He was truly a legend in his own time and for a long time afterwards. He thoroughly destroyed everyone who challenged him, and he thought of himself as being invincible. He decided training was unnecessary and began to drink heavily and carouse around, boasting he was unbeatable. But a young man who had been weak and sickly most of his young life decided to go into serious training and challenge the great Sullivan. His name was Jim Corbett, referred to mockingly as "Gentleman Jim." While he was training, Sullivan was having a good time and boasting he would demolish "Gentleman Jim" with one punch. When at last they met in the ring, the bout went on and on, round after round. In the end, Sullivan lay flat on his back and "Gentleman Jim" was champion of the world.

When at last Sullivan came around, he stood up in the ring and apologized to the world for what he had become, and he spent the rest of his life speaking to young and old alike about the dangers of drink and the need for a disciplined life. Self-control and perseverance suggest that the Christian life is a life-long commitment to the Lord; self-control under Christ's leadership and perseverance to the end.

E. GODLINESS. There is a natural progression in this formula Peter gives us. Faith plus virtue plus knowledge added to self-control and perseverance result in godliness, or God-likeness. For all these qualities or attributes are found in God, and by grace He communicates them to us. But the true expression of godliness in our lives is seen in kindness and, beyond that, in agape love. So, the final step in the pathway to assurance is right at this point.

F. Finally, Peter pleads for BROTHER KINDNESS and LOVE. If faith is the foundation, then love is the highest expression of the Christian life and the surest sign we have Christ in our hearts. John joins with Peter in insisting this is the true mark of a believer, and the way we may know beyond doubt we belong to Christ. The word for kindness is simply "philadelphia." This is an attitude which expresses itself in an outgoing, outreaching life to people all around us. It will be tested, even severely at times, but it is God's way of showing His general kindness to all. You get the impression with some Christians that they are so close to the Lord they don't have time for people. Look at Jesus - so close to the Father, yet always ready to be with and minister to people of all degree.

Love, the kind described here, is one step beyond that. It is a sacrificial love for us while we were yet sinners. John put it this way: "This is the message you have heard from the beginning, that we should love one another. By this we know love because He laid down his life for us, and we ought to lay down our lives for the brethren."

So there it is. No, real and true assurance does not come easy, but when you have it, it is a priceless treasure. Do you have this assurance? Walk this pathway, try this formula, and you will find it. And as you continue on this way, your assurance will grow and grow until faith gives way to sight.

One of the values of the blessed sacrament the Lord's Supper in the Christian's life is that it affords an opportunity to reflect and examine ourselves. As we do this, the Holy Spirit will enable us to see the areas of weakness in our walk with the Lord, convict us of our need of repentance, and motivate us towards this pathway of assurance.

For Discussion and Reflection

1. How can you apply Peter's formula as described above to your life? Make a list of specific steps that you can take to begin weaving into your life your own tapestry of faith, virtue, knowledge, self-control and perseverance, godliness, and brother kindness and love.

2. Forgiveness is key to becoming a strong and effective believer. How do you handle forgiveness in your life, both as the recipient and as the giver?

3. How is your life fruitful in terms of service to God?

4. How do you respond when your efforts of "brother love" are rebuffed? What can you draw upon from Peter's teaching to give you strength in these situations?

5. What are your areas of weakness in your walk with the Lord? What steps can you take to strengthen these weaknesses?

Holy Bible: God's Voice to Man

2 Peter 1:1-21

There is one great dividing issue before the Church in our day. All other divisions and debates have their origin in this one, and all pale into relatively unimportant side issues compared to this one great issue. All matters of argument, all debates, and all divisions come into focus at the point of the place and authority of the Bible. Is it what the historic documents of the Church claim for it - the Word of God written, the infallible rule of faith and life - or is it something less, as so many now claim? This was the basic issue of the Reformation and remains the basic issue in the Church to this very day.

The importance of this matter cannot be over emphasized, for the answer to the question, "What is the Bible?" will determine the answer to all other religious questions, such as, "Who is God?" "What has He done?" "What is the Church?" "What am I to believe?" "How am I to live?" Many trace the beginnings of the decline in faith and the rapid decline of the Church in the past two decades to an undermining of man's faith in the Bible as the Word of God. There is much validity in this contention.

In the past, there has always been much debate in the Church over interpretation of the Bible, but nearly always in the context of faith; that is to say, whatever divisions and battles were fought, they were not fought over the presupposition that the Bible is in fact the voice of God speaking to man. This is no longer true. The real battles of belief in our time are joined at this point: "Is the Bible the true and authentic voice of God revealing Himself to man, or is it primarily a work of man in which we discover man's ideas and thoughts about God?" Between the two positions there lies a great gulf fixed which cannot be crossed or harmonized except by a capitulation to unbelief or else a coming to faith on the part of unbelief.

At the time of the Reformation, the battle was joined at this point: only the Church may interpret the meaning of the Bible. So sure was the medieval Church of this mistaken idea that only the clergy had access to the Bible, and the penalty for translating the Bible into the common tongue of the people was death. The most notable martyrs to this terrible error were Tyndale and Wycliff. What is at stake is this: "Do we have a reliable, authentic, powerful self-revelation of God to man (through human channels to be sure) or not?" If we do have such a document, then a saving relationship with the Living God is possible, and man may have a proper understanding of himself, a knowledge of his past and his destiny, and hope that is sure and unfailing. If in the Bible we have something less than such a document, then we have no assurance whatsoever that we know anything about God or ourselves, and whatever hope we have is purely an invention to forestall despair.

Simon Peter, the great apostle of the early Church, had certain things to say to the young Church about the Scriptures. Primarily, he was talking about the Old Testament, but he did favorably compare the writings of Paul, another apostle, with the Old Testament Scriptures. However, the principles of truth about the Scriptures which we discover in his writings apply even more to the New Testament. In this short passage of Scripture, we discover one of the most helpful sections in all the Bible which relates to the question before us: "What is the Bible? Is it really the voice of God to man?"

THE FIRST THING Peter says about the Scriptures is that they are not a collection of "cunningly devised fables" (NKJV); or, as we would say, they are not fairy tales. One of the major accusations against the Bible is that it is made up of myths and legends and half-true tales preserved from the past. The stories may contain some truth, or at least they suggest universal truth, but the stories themselves are not true. They go on to say by way of illustration that Isaiah did not really predict certain events, but an unknown prophet who lived much later, using Isaiah's name, wrote about things that had already happened and pretended it was prophecy. Or you may hear something like this: The story of Jonah is not really true, but the point of the story is what really counts. Also, you will hear people say Jesus did not really rise from the dead, but He lives in the hearts of those who love Him." Against this accusation of myth and legend we have the clear words of Peter, "We did not follow cleverly devised myths."

We believe that God does not speak the truth through legends and myths, but rather His Word is the accurate report of truth as it happened in history and as it applies to us today. Much of the Bible was written by actual eyewitnesses to the events recorded, or to whom the Lord spoke His word. Anytime you hear or read something which casts doubts upon the truth of the Bible, even though these things may be spoken or written by ministers or theologians, you may be sure God is not speaking through such people.

ANOTHER GREAT TRUTH ABOUT THE BIBLE is that it all revolves about and centers in Jesus Christ. Peter says that it is through the study of the Scripture that Jesus Christ will become a living, shining reality in your own life. Many people today want shortcuts to Christianity. They want to know and have Jesus without the discipline of studying and knowing the Word of God. This simply cannot be done. No experience can replace the Bible. On the contrary, all our experiences must be judged by the Bible and not the other way around. All the Bible from Genesis through Malachi was in preparation for and prophetic of Jesus Christ. He is in Himself the fulfillment of the law and the prophets. All the Bible from Matthew through Revelation tells about Jesus Christ, and it interprets the meaning of His life and teachings. It tells us that in Him all history has its focus and meaning. You simply cannot separate Jesus Christ from the Bible. He is what the Bible is all about. In the Bible alone do we have any record of His life and words. In the Bible alone do we have the authentic plan of salvation presented for people to understand and receive.

As wonderful as it may be to walk where Jesus walked and to see the Holy Land of His birth and life, remember that the Bible is the true "land of Jesus," and a walk of faith through its pages will bring you much closer to Jesus Christ than a lifetime lived in Israel. If Jesus Christ is not real to you, it is probably because you have neglected His Word. If you seem to have lost touch with Him, it is likely you have lost touch with the Bible. If you yearn for Him to be a living Lord and very present and powerful Savior, then you must go to the Bible. You must feed upon His Word, then you will discover that the written word leads you to the Living Word.

FINALLY, PETER TELLS US that the Bible came to us from men inspired by the Holy Spirit. The Living Bible translates this last verse this way: "No prophecy recorded in Scripture was ever thought up by the prophet himself; it was the Holy

Spirit within those godly men who gave them true messages from God." Notice what this says about the Bible. (1) It says men spoke. No one denies that the Bible was written by men. It was written by many different men who lived over a span of at least fifteen hundred years. These men were human beings just as you and I are. They were fallible men, and not perfect. How, then, could sinful fallible man write the infallible Word of God? This same verse which tells us that men wrote the Bible also (2) tells us that what they wrote was prompted by the Holy Spirit. A very literal translation of this sentence tells us that they were borne along by the Spirit as a ship is carried along by the wind. In reporting what they had seen and heard and experienced, those men were being inspired by God Himself to faithfully record the timeless revelation of Himself for all mankind. (3) As a result, what they said and wrote was from God. Thus, their word became God's Word, and their role was one of being channels and instruments through which God revealed Himself to mankind.

Jesus Christ believed in the full inspiration of the Scriptures of the Old Testament. He placed His stamp of approval on all that was written. He said of the Old Testament, "You search the Scriptures because you think that in them you have eternal life; and it is they that bear witness about me" (John 5:39). Jesus and the inspired apostles who wrote of Him bore witness that the Bible was the Word of God.

What does all this mean to you and for you?

3. HOLY BIBLE: GOD'S VOICE TO MAN

Most of you agree with what I have said and believe the Bible is the Word of God. So, why bother to talk about it?

If we really believe the Bible is the Word of God, if we accept its authority over us - and not just with lip service - how dare we continue to ignore and reject its teachings and its commands? You say you accept the Bible as God's Word over your life; then what are you doing about evangelism? How excited are you about missions? Why are you neither teaching nor attending a Sunday school class? Why do you continue to excuse yourself from any active form of Christian service or Christian living? How can you continue to look down on other people who are not of your own social status or race? How can you excuse your self-righteousness and your lack of real love for the brethren?

What I am trying to say is that it is not enough to say you believe the Bible is the Word of God. You must place yourself under its authority and judge your life by it – and be willing to change your attitudes and your activities. In the declining years of the Kingdom, when the temple of God was being repaired, an amazing thing happened. A copy of the law of God was discovered. The Bible had been lost and neglected for many years in Judah until that time. This lost book was brought to the king who read it, who in turn read it to the people. When the king and the people realized how far astray they had gone from God, they mourned and wept before the Lord, and a real revival of truth, faith, and religion broke out in the land. O that God's Word would be rediscovered in this Church, not only as a sacred and revered treasure, but as a living, ruling power over our lives. O that God would break us before Him and bring to pass a great outpouring of His Holy Spirit upon us, that His Word would become for each of us what it was intended to be: THE VOICE OF GOD TO MAN.

For Discussion and Reflection

If you accept the Bible as God's Word over your life, then consider these questions.

1. In what ways do you practice evangelism in your daily life?

2. Do you actively engage in any form of Christian outreach or mission work? If not, how can you incorporate this aspect of Christian living into your life? If you are already involved, can you identify ways in which you might expand upon your efforts?

3. Do you regularly attend Sunday school or set aside time each day for study and prayer? If not, thoughtfully consider why regular study and prayer are not part of your routine. Then, work out a plan for gradually adding both into your schedule.

4. Meditate on 2 Peter 1:3 for a few minutes. What are the boundaries "everything we need for life and godliness" (Christian Standard Bible)? What does "knowing God" have to do with this promise?

5. Continuing to reflect upon 2 Peter 1:3, what does it mean for you personally to be called "by his own glory and goodness" (CSB)? How does God's glory, goodness, and presence affect how you walk through your life?

4

Holy Bible: Fact or Fable?

2 Peter 1:12-21

In the late spring of 1808, the USS Topaz dropped anchor in the bay of a small and isolated island in the South Pacific. The name of that island was called Pitcairn. You may remember that name from one of the most famous - or infamous - incidents in naval history. Several years before the Topaz visited that island, it became well known because that was the final destination of the mutineers who took over the British ship Bounty. These men set Captain Bligh and his loyal followers adrift in an open life boat. They managed to sail and row 2,300 miles and finally reached land safely on an island just off the coast of Australia, and from there they returned to England with their report of the mutiny on the Bounty.

The mutineers, led by the first mate Christian, realized they would be hunted down, and so they sailed the Bounty to this little isolated island, sank their ship just off the coast, then made their way to land and attempted to establish a colony. There were nine British sailors, six Polynesian men, and eleven Polynesian women, one of whom was only 15 years old. One of the sailors discovered a way of making alcohol and soon the combination of drunkenness, competition over the women, and the absence of any semblance of law and order produced violence, rape, and murder. The colony became a virtual cesspool of vice and corruption. Christian himself was murdered by one of his own men. The British sailors and the Polynesian men fought repeatedly, and in the end only one British sailor, Alexander Smith, survived.

    Then an amazing thing happened. Smith was going through some of the chests that had been saved when the Bounty was sunk, and he discovered a Bible. He began to read it and soon came to saving faith in Jesus Christ. He set out to teach to others the truths he had found in God's Word. What a hopeless task it would be. How could one man possibly rescue such a colony of criminals? But when the Topaz dropped anchor in that lonely bay, and when the captain and part of the crew went ashore with deep apprehension of what thy might find, much to their amazement they found a thriving, prosperous Christian community. Alcohol had been completely banished and there was no jail or need for one, for there was no crime. There was no mental institution, but there was a church, a school, and an island full of believers who had rebuilt their lives individually and collectively around the Word of God. Truly, the discovery of the Bible had transformed that little community.

That was not the first time such a glorious transformation had taken place in history. One great example of this was the transformation that took place in Colonial America as a result of the Great Awakening. Contrary to what some think, about two or three generations after the initial colonization of New England, the Mid-Atlantic, and the coastal South, spiritual life had sunk to a low ebb in all these colonies. Less than twenty percent of the population attended church of any kind, and many of the churches had fallen victim to Unitarianism, which had undermined the authority and truth of the Bible as the guiding force in the lives of the American colonies. Then came the widespread revivals of the Great Awakening, and true biblical Christianity became the heart beat of America and the foundation for the emergence of the greatest republic the world has ever known.

Another example is shown in 2 Chronicles 34-35 and 2 Kings 22-23, where we have one of the most powerful testimonies to the life-changing and nation-changing power of the Bible ever recorded. Judah had sunk to her lowest point spiritually, politically, and militarily in all her long history. Idolatry was rampant. The temple was neglected and in ruins. The Word of God sent through Moses and other prophets was abandoned and forgotten. For several generations, the Bible was a lost book. Then a new young king named Josiah ascended the throne of Judah at the tender age of eight years. When he was sixteen years old, he began to seek the Lord. When he was only twenty, he instituted a program of reform in Judah which included the banishment of idolatry and an all-out effort to restore the ruined Temple of God. It was during this latter effort that a copy of God's lost Word was found in the rubble of the temple. When this book was brought and read to the king and his court, the effects were dramatic and electrifying! A spirit of repentance fell upon the young king and all his court. A true, powerful, and sweeping spiritual revival broke out in Judah, led by this godly young man. True biblical and spiritual worship replaced the blasphemous worship current in Judah. There was weeping and repentance throughout the land, and the king made a national covenant that Judah would commit itself to obey the law of God in every respect. The holy ordinance of the Passover would be observed once more. For the rest of Josiah's young life (he died at age 39), Judah honored and served God. His epitaph reads like this: "Before him there was no king like him, who turned to the LORD with all his heart and with all his soul and with all his might, according to all the Law of Moses, nor did any like him arise after him" (2 Kings 23:25).

    Now do you understand why a man on death row who wanted to leave a final charge and encouragement to God's people after his own demise would take the time to simply remind his beloved flock that they had in their hands the very Word of God written? It was Simon Peter's last words to the Church of the Lord, and he wanted to remind them that it was by God's Word that they were established in the Truth, which afforded them an abundant entrance into the Kingdom of God. This abiding truth is none other than what you, too, have before you, in your hands this very day: God's Word; forever settled in the heavens and revealed fully and inerrantly in the written Scriptures of the Old and New Testaments.

I. Peter's defense of the Bible

By the time Peter wrote this last short letter, some very serious errors and heresies had infiltrated the Church. There were all sorts of strange and imaginary tales which were being circulated among the Church as sober truths. Some were teaching that Jesus was only a mere man. Others taught He was an angelic being, but not God. Still others contended that Jesus was true deity, but He only took on a human appearance of mankind. The sad thing is that these heresies are still around and are circulated once more as alternatives to the true Gospel. It must have grieved and angered Peter and the other surviving apostles to hear such nonsense being passed off as truth by people who had never known, seen, or heard Jesus.

He wrote of all these misleading teachings, "For we did not follow cleverly devised myths when we made known to you the power and coming of our Lord Jesus Christ, but we were eyewitnesses of his majesty." This sounds so very much like the way the apostle John began one of his last letters to the Church when he wrote, "That which was from the beginning, which we have heard, which we have seen with our eyes, which we looked upon and have touched with our hands, concerning the word of life…that which we have seen and heard we proclaim also to you" (I John 1:1, 3).

II. The focal point of all Scripture is our Lord Jesus Christ

At this point, you get the idea that these men who were eyewitnesses of Christ's life, death, resurrection, and ascension were trying to combat all these strange heresies by reminding their congregations, "We were there when it happened. We don't need to make up strange and corrupting stories about our Lord."

Peter went on to say that their personal experiences with the Lord Jesus were exactly what the Scriptures of the Old Testament had prophesied of Him. Not only this, but they, the apostles, had actually heard the voice of God coming from the glory of heaven and saying of Jesus, "This is my beloved Son, with whom I am well pleased." So the things written of the coming Messiah were confirmed by His life and ministry to which the Father testified as a voice from heaven, and to which these eye witnesses also bore their witness. And as for the nature of the written word, "Men spoke from God as they were carried along by the Holy Spirit." The word 'carried' or 'moved' is the same word in the Greek language used to describe a ship being driven by the wind.

Peter here also insists that the Scripture means what God Himself says it means. The whole idea that the Bible may mean anything fallen human beings want it to mean is dismissed by these words: "No prophecy of Scripture comes from someone's own interpretation. For no prophecy was ever produced by the will of man." This does not restrict us from trying to understand the Word. In fact, it encourages us to do so. But the point the great Reformers made is that Scripture must and does interpret itself. If you want to understand any one part of Scripture, it must be understood in light of the whole. Let me give an illustration of this. Your understanding of John 3:16 must be consistent with the whole chapter and, indeed, the whole book of John and all of the Bible. The next time you read or quote John 3:16, read along with that verse John 15:16 and John 17:6, and you will see what I mean.

III. The powerful effects of God's Word

If you were dying today or tomorrow, what would you want to pass on to your family that would sustain and guide them throughout the rest of their lives? Enough income to live on? Yes, but is that enough? The house and land? Yes, but does that go far enough? Let me tell you what I want to pass on to you and to my family above everything else...the Bible. Oh, I know all of you have plenty of Bibles in your homes, but that's not what I mean. I want to pass on to you a love for God's Word, a hunger for it, and above all a life-sustaining confidence in the Bible as God's Word.

If I can somehow give you that and convince you that what God has to say is more important than anything else you will ever know, I will know my task on earth and in Christ's Church is complete. I will have given you something that will endure all tests and trials and will guide you safely home.

Peter was still a work in process when he wrote these words, but he had come a long, long way from the day Christ met him and called him to become His disciple. Notice some of the milestones along that way.

> *Depart from me, for I am a sinful man, O Lord.¹ Lord, if it is you, command me to come to you on the water.* This was immediately followed by: *Lord, save me!² You are the Christ, the Son of the living God.³ See, we have left everything and followed you. What then will we have?⁴ Lord...I will lay down my life for You.⁵ I am not [one of His disciples].⁶ I do not know the man.⁷ Lord, you know everything; you know that I love you.⁸ There is no other name under heaven given among men by which we must be saved.⁹*

But even a forgiven, growing, maturing Christian is not perfect, for after all this, Peter, under pressure from other believers, denied his oneness with Gentile believers by separating himself from them when he criticized Jewish Christians for having fellowship with them. Paul, in loving boldness, had to rebuke him publicly and to his face. How do you suppose this same man could write both epistles which bear his name? I think the answer is simply this: God doesn't give up on believers, even when they stumble. As they abide in His Word and are renewed by the Holy Spirit, they are restored and strengthened. In the final verses in this passage, Peter obviously alludes to his own experiences with the Lord. But the whole idea was to leave behind him, after his death, a testimony that would help believers to know and experience the same truths. So, do you want to know more and more of your Lord, and experience more and more of His grace and goodness? Then stay in the Word and seek the illuminating power of the Holy Spirit as you compare Scripture with Scripture and thereby grow both in your knowledge of and likeness to the Lord Jesus Christ. Then you, too, will live as Peter lived, and face death with the same calm, optimistic expectation of seeing Your precious Lord in Heaven.

For Discussion and Reflection

1. If you were dying today or tomorrow, what would you want to pass on to your family that would sustain and guide them throughout the rest of their lives?

2. If you found yourself in a situation similar to Alexander Smith's, how would you begin the process of drawing non-believers to Christ? Consider the reality of your life. How do you witness for Christ in the circles you travel from day to day?

3. How do you respond when asked about the heresies being promoted within our churches today?

4. As is the case with all of us, Peter's spiritual growth was marked by ups and downs. Can you identify milestones in your growth as a Christian?

5. "Men spoke from God as they were carried along by the Holy Spirit." (2 Peter 1:31) As discussed above, the word 'carried' or 'moved' is the same word in the Greek language used to describe a ship being driven by the wind. Spend some time reflecting upon this image. Then, in light of this definition, reconsider those situations in your life for which you seek "movement" or "motivation." Does the image help inspire or energize you?

[1] Luke 5:8
[2] Matthew 14:28, 30
[3] Matthew 16:16
[4] Matthew 19:27
[5] John 13:38
[6] John 18:17, 25
[7] Matthew 26:72, 74
[8] John 21:17
[9] Acts 4:12

5

HOLY BIBLE: MORE THAN A LONG AND RICH HERITAGE

2 Peter 1:12-21

Simon Peter, writing just before his execution, wrote this final short letter so that his loved ones, the sheep Christ had given him to feed and shepherd, might have all they would need to endure the loss of their beloved leader and the trials they, too, would shortly face. Over and over again, he mentioned the importance of knowledge as a bulwark against the assaults they would soon face.

"Since I know that the putting off of my body will be soon…I will make every effort so that after my departure you may be able at any time to recall these things" is the way Peter expressed it.

We are a people who have taken our stand, claiming that we believe the Bible is truly God's Word. To those who would challenge its authority or authenticity, we have said, "We will take our stand on the Bible, God's Word." Even in the formation of the Presbyterian Church in America (PCA), we felt it was necessary to separate ourselves from a long and rich heritage, because we saw the denomination we loved slipping away from that confidence in the Bible.

However, this battle still rages, and we cannot simply say, "We've taken our stand" and let it go at that. As a pastor who loves God's people, and as a shepherd Christ has placed in His church, I feel compelled to continue to raise the issue. Do we really believe the Bible is God's Word, God revealing Himself and His will to us? It would seem that people who truly believe this would always be seeking to know and understand what God has said, and that this desire would be the highest priority. I would think that people who truly believe the Bible is God's inspired and inerrant book would eagerly seek for every opportunity to hear and study His Word. Yet even among those of us who take this stand, we see an alarming indifference towards Sunday school and serious in-depth Bible study. Have a church supper or a barbeque and people will come in droves. Have a serious study of God's Word, and the same folks stay away in droves and have "good reasons" why this is unimportant.

Yet in this book we claim to believe, God tells us who He is and who we are. He reveals the way of salvation and offers a philosophy of life that is unshakeable. He gives us His law and His grace. He tells us how the world began and how it will end; where we came from and where we're going. In places, this book is amazingly simple,

5. HOLY BIBLE: MORE THAN A LONG AND RICH HERITAGE

and in others amazingly complex, and God wants us to know both the simple and the difficult.

So, what does the dying Simon Peter say about this book we take so lightly, or leave so easily?

I. The Bible is not a collection of cunning fables, but an eyewitness account by faithful men.

One of the major accusations against the Bible, and this comes in many forms, is that the Bible is simply a product of the mind of man; a collection of ancient myths and legends with no historical foundation. Those who take this position in a benevolent or even benign way would charitably say that these stories suggest some universal truths, but they are certainly not accurate accounts of the past, nor are they in any way supernaturally inspired. When they are confronted with the amazing prophecies which came to pass, they shrug off these things by saying they were written after the fact, and then claimed to be written as prophecy foretelling future events.

Such people not only deny such stories as the creation of the world, the universal flood of Noah's time, the exodus from Egypt and other events, but they will deny the resurrection of Jesus Christ from the dead, and some even go so far as to say Jesus never existed.

Against these unfounded accusations of myth and legend, we have these clear words from Simon Peter, as if anticipating the denials of unbelievers: "we did not follow cleverly devised myths when we made known to you the power and coming of our Lord Jesus Christ, but we were eyewitnesses of his majesty." He went on to claim, "For when he received honor and glory from God the Father, and the voice was borne to him by the Majestic Glory, 'This is my beloved Son, with whom I am well pleased,' we ourselves heard this very voice borne from heaven, for we were with him on the holy mountain."

We also affirm the same principle concerning the entire Bible. God did not speak through fanciful made-up myths and legends, but rather through men who spoke from Him as they were carried along by the Holy Spirit to accurately report the events of redemptive history and explain their meaning. In fact, it is absolutely amazing how modern archeology has abundantly supported the facts reported in the Bible.

So, the Bible is true; it came from God. What is it all about and how does that affect you and me?

II. The whole Bible from Genesis through Revelation centers in the person and work of Jesus Christ.

The Living Bible says that through the study of Scripture, Jesus Christ becomes a living and shining reality in your life. Many people want shortcuts in their Christian life. They want to experience the reality of Jesus Christ without the discipline of regular and demanding study of God's Word and a commitment to serious praying. Camp, mission trips, concerts, and similar experiences,

5. HOLY BIBLE: MORE THAN A LONG AND RICH HERITAGE

while fun and helpful, cannot replace regular and faithful study of God's Word. No experience or heartwarming inner glow can take the place of Scripture. In fact, any religious experience ought to be measured and judged by how much it points you to the Lord's revelation in the Bible.

All the Old Testament from Genesis through Malachi was prophetic of and preparatory for the coming of the Lord Jesus Christ into the world. After His resurrection, Jesus met with His disciples and walked them through the whole Old Testament, showing how it spoke of Him. All the New Testament from Matthew through Revelation presents Christ and explains the meaning of His coming. It tells us that He came, why He came, and why He is sure to return. You cannot separate Jesus from the Bible, or the Bible from Him. He is what it is all about. Furthermore, it forces you to deal with Him in your life, to make basic decisions concerning Him. He will not be ignored, and you do so at the peril of your immortal soul.

Some people like to make pilgrimages to the land where Jesus lived His earthly life. They testify how thrilling it is to walk where He walked. But the Bible is the real land of Jesus. Bishop Pike, one of the liberal leaders of the Episcopal Church in the 1950s-'60s, lost his faith in Christianity. He had decided the Bible was not true, so he went to Israel to try to find his lost faith in the wilderness of Judea. They found his dead body in the wilderness, but there is no evidence that Bishop Pike recovered his lost faith. Once you leave the Bible, there is no other place to seek and find Jesus Christ.

If you seem to be out of touch with God, it is because you have lost touch with His Word. It is through the written Word that the Holy Spirit brings you to know and experience Jesus Christ in your life.

III. Finally, Peter tells us that the Bible was not a human invention, but men spoke from God as they were carried along by the Holy Spirit.

Again, the Living Bible is helpful in our understanding of verse 21. "No prophecy recorded in Scripture was ever thought up by the prophet himself, but it was the Holy Spirit within these godly men who gave them true messages from God." Note what is said about the Bible.

(1) Men spoke. No one denies that the Bible was actually written by human beings. In fact, men who lived over a period of almost 1,700 years wrote the Bible. These men were not perfect or in themselves infallible. So, how could all these sinful men who lived hundreds and even thousands of years apart write a book that is so unified and perfect? The text tells us.

(2) "They spoke as they were carried along by the Holy Spirit." The language is graphic. They were like sailing ships with the sails unfurled, and the wind of the Holy Spirit filled those sails and moved them along. Another figure of speech meets us in the book of Judges. The Holy Spirit clothed Himself with those He chose to lead God's people.

Were these men robots? No! They were living, breathing men, but men chosen by God to receive and record His revelation and His salvation through Christ the Living Word. As a result, (3) what they said and wrote was of God and was His Word.

      Think about it. That Bible you hold in your hand and treat so lightly contains in it all you ever need to know, and more than you can ever fully comprehend about God, life, yourself, how to be forgiven, and how to get to heaven. Don't you understand that while so many people in this world have never seen a Bible or heard its message, we who have this blessed book will be held accountable by God for what we do with it? I challenge you today, and I plead with you today. Take the word of a man on death row who wanted to make sure his loved ones would get to heaven. Take the word of a pastor who loves you and would give up anything including life itself for you. The Bible is the voice of God speaking to your mind and heart. Are you listening?

For Discussion and Reflection

1. Do you seek opportunities for in-depth study of the Bible, such as attendance at Sunday school or educational offerings at your church? If not, reflect seriously upon your reasons for bypassing these opportunities to deepen your understanding of God's Word. What is keeping you from drawing closer to God through knowledge of His Word?

2. Do you make time each day to spend in prayer with our Lord? If not, take this moment to discern the reasons that you pull away rather than drawing nearer to Him. What can you do to change this?

3. In what ways do the Scriptures act for you as "a lamp shining in a dark place"? (2 Peter 1:19) What does the darkness represent? What does the light represent?

4. In some translations, Peter describes his body as a 'tent' or 'tabernacle' (2 Peter 1:13). How do these descriptions change the way you think of your physical body?

5. "Men spoke from God as they were carried along by the Holy Spirit." (2 Peter 1:21) How does the image of these holy men as ships and the Holy Spirit as the wind filling their sails help you understand the concept of the divine authorship of the Bible? Consider, too, the image from 2 Timothy 3:16 of Scripture being "breathed" by God (from the Greek pneuma, 'spirit' means 'breath' or 'wind'). Does this change or enhance your understanding of this concept?

6

DANGER: FALSE TEACHERS AHEAD

2 Peter 2:1-22

These words from 2 Peter 2 may not be what many would expect from a man facing death. Yet, if you were facing death and knew of a terrible danger facing your loved ones of which they seemed to be unaware, wouldn't you want to warn them? Here we find Simon Peter more concerned about the false teachers who were beginning to spread their dangerous doctrines throughout the Church than he was about the dangers of persecution and death through which the Church most shortly go.

False teachers or false prophets? You've got to be kidding! That has a medieval ring to it, or suggests a Salem witch hunt by intolerant people. But Jesus had also warned against the same danger and Peter thought this warning was so important that it took up over a third of his last letter. Go back to the teaching of Jesus, and you will find that

He spoke often and seriously about false teachers or false prophets. A prophet in the biblical sense was not so much one who predicted the future, but one who claimed to have messages from God about the past, present, and future. Those who claim to represent God and speak His Word, but in reality speak falsely in His name, do far more harm to the Church in the long run than all the Neros and Hitlers and other persecutors who have ever lived.

      This is a very difficult subject to bring before you for four reasons. (1) There are preachers who label anyone who disagrees with their own interpretation of Scripture a false teacher. (2) Because of the erosion of biblical thinking which has taken place over the last several decades, most people think truth is relative. There is no such thing as good and bad, righteousness and evil. In this age of misguided toleration, everyone is entitled to their own ideas and life style, and there is no set standard of right and wrong. In fact, in the minds of many, the only wrong thing is for you to think and say there are some things which are right and some things wrong. (3) Even all true believers are beset every day with temptations to sin the same sorts of sins with which unbelievers are faced. When believers deal with these temptations and may even fall at some point, the inclination is to write themselves and others off, and feel that because they sin in thought and/or deed, they are without hope. Satan obviously loves to afflict believers with their own faults and failures to drive them away from Christ and the cross. (4) There was obviously a lot going on in the first century Church of which we know very little, and yet we are apt to read into the words of Scripture applications and meanings which are not consistent with the context.

However, for those who take the Bible seriously, we simply cannot ignore the fact that the Scriptures speak often and very harshly about false teachers and false prophets and their misguided followers. The chief architects of Israel's decline and eventual destruction were false prophets; men who claimed to bring true messages from God, but instead led the people into sin, idolatry, and eventual judgment.

Jesus warned His disciples over and over again about false prophets, as did all the writers of the New Testament. He called them wolves in sheep's clothing. One of the common threads which runs through all these warnings is that they would appear on the scene with increasing frequency as the end times draw near. Peter put it this way: "There were false prophets among the people, even as there will be false teachers among you ... and many will follow their destructive ways ..." (KJV). This is true of every generation, and none more than our own.

I. Who are these false teachers and how will we know who they are?

When Peter used this term, he was undoubtedly echoing the warnings of Jesus when He said: "Beware of false prophets, who come to you in sheep's clothing but inwardly are ravenous wolves ..." Those are strong and sobering words. Add to these the warnings of the apostle Paul when he said: "[Satan's] servants disguise themselves as servants of righteousness" (2 Corinthians 11:15). What did Jesus mean? What did Paul mean? What did Peter mean?

(1) First, false teachers never appear to be false ... at first. They are "nice" people who are able to convince many people and, at times, even most people. A wolf pretending to be a sheep would have to look very, very much like a sheep to fool anyone. Satan's ambassadors would have to sound very, very much like a true minister to gain an audience.

Our idea of a false teacher would be an obvious villain but, according to Jesus and His disciples, that would hardly suit the case. In fact, the false teachers of Israel were wildly popular, while God's true prophets were hated, stoned, and murdered in many cruel ways, and at best were imprisoned. So today, some of the most honored and sought-after religious speakers on the conference and campus circuit are those who ridicule the Christian faith and scorn the Bible. They promote a revival of paganism and pagan morality in the name of tolerance and the new morality. Or else they promote Christianity as just another form of fun and entertainment as a substitute for biblical and truly spiritual worship.

Thus, the historical custom of honoring the false prophet is carried on today as well as in the past. Homosexual priests, pastors, and even

6. DANGER: FALSE TEACHERS AHEAD

bishops are being ordained and exalted to the highest positions in some church bodies, and these sins are being actively promoted and condoned as acceptable to God and even to be encouraged in the churches. This is no laughing matter, and the danger is real. The Lord said many would be led astray by their evil teaching.

(2) We must press the question further and ask, "How will we know and recognize such people?" Peter refers to them in this passage as "even denying the Master." Note carefully these words: *denying the Master*. The critics might ask, "How could a man who denied his Lord under pressure dare accuse someone else of denying the Lord?" The answer is found in the magnitude of the problems to which Peter refers. This was not just a matter of some people getting into moral failures. This was a widespread organized effort to corrupt Christianity with the infusion of pagan doctrines and practices. Paul probably alludes to the same problem when he mentioned that some people were actually saying, "The more we sin, the more grace abounds." Temple prostitution was widely practiced in the pagan world of the Greco-Roman Empire, and this also involved homosexual prostitution which was widely practiced also. This may account for Peter's reference to Sodom and Gomorrah.

What we see happening in the modern Church was unthinkable a few years ago. Those promoting such things must be labeled as false prophets even if they hold the title of 'bishop' in an erstwhile biblical denomination. At the same time, we too must guard ourselves against two very dangerous sins, the first being that we would become too lax in our own attitudes and behavior. Very humbly, we should review what our Lord had to say in His Sermon on the Mount about the sinfulness of immoral thoughts and words, and acknowledge as we did in reading these words from Psalm 130: "If you, O Lord should mark iniquities, O Lord who could stand?" The second being that we would forget that no matter how much we might hate the sin, we must not hate the sinners, but earnestly pray for them. Very few on the Christian scene today have been more outspoken in denouncing such sins as abortion and homosexuality than Dr. James Kennedy, and few, if any, have shown more sincere and effective efforts to minister to those trapped in these sinful patterns. O that the same things could be said of every congregation of Christ's Church.

  The false prophet would never begin by flatly denying the Scripture. More likely, he would take Satan's route when he tempted Eve, saying, "Did God really say that? Was He really born of a virgin and why is that important anyway? All those miracles we read about, wasn't that just a way of saying He was a loving person? How could He be sinless, anymore than all of us are sinless? Why talk about the death and, even worse, the blood of Christ; we don't need a slaughter-house religion. The Resurrection? Well, yes, He lives on in the hearts of His disciples. Would a loving God ever really send anyone to hell?" Little by little, confusion

6. DANGER: FALSE TEACHERS AHEAD

replaces knowledge, and doubt replaces faith. "Creation in the space of six days by the word and act of God? Nonsense; we all know it wasn't that way." So in the end, the Bible is either ridiculed or rejected for the so-called wisdom of man.

But there is another way to deny the Lord, and this is even more dangerous, especially for folks who believe the Bible is truly God's Word. One may claim to believe the Bible and all it teaches, yet live by the standards of the culture in which we find ourselves. We may forget that much of the Christian world lives in poverty and fear of oppression, while we enjoy an opulent lifestyle and compromise with the world so much it has nothing to fear from us. This is a far more insidious and dangerous form of error. How terribly sad it is for those who claim true faith to deny that faith by deed and lifestyle. In His Sermon on the Mount, Jesus described the false prophet as one who failed to teach that the Kingdom of God is entered by a narrow gate and leads along a steep and difficult path. So, the false prophet is one who ignores sin and the need of repentance, and the necessity of a living holy life, and preaches a cheap and easy grace that costs nothing and requires nothing. If you omit self-denial and cross-bearing, you cut the heart and soul out of the teaching of Jesus.

Our Lord taught the absolute necessity of new birth, and that new birth leads to a new way of living. Most of us attempt to soften this straight and hard line. We pad the rough edges and take out of context so much of our Lord's teachings in order to make it acceptable and pleasant to the ears of the unconverted. Isn't that where we are in the Church today?

II. The fate of the false prophets

There is nothing pleasant in the words of this dying man as he describes the awful consequences and the end of such people. Peter describes their judgment in terms of the flood in Noah's day and the fiery end of Sodom and Gomorrah. That's pretty grim, but the catalog of their destructive influence on the Church makes their end both just and inevitable. In Peter's words, they are wells without water, clouds without rain, for whom is reserved the blackness of darkness forever.

III. The destructive influence of the false prophets

The even greater tragedy is their influence on multitudes. Jesus said, "Many will say to me, 'Lord, Lord, did we not prophesy in your name, and cast out demons in your name, and do many mighty works in your name?' And then will I declare to them, 'I never knew you; depart from me, you workers of lawlessness'" (Matthew 7:22-23). Peter warned that these false prophets were in it for the profit and for personal satisfaction. He said they were proud, greedy, and lustful. So as a dying man, Peter felt a need to include this warning in his last letter out of death row.

This was his way of saying that false teachers are one of the greatest dangers facing believers.

There are many evils and dangers at every turn for believers, but few, if any, are more deadly than this.

IV. How will we know the true from the false?

There is a word of advice from Isaiah, a true prophet of God. When he was asked this question, he said, "To the law and the testimony: if they speak not according to this word, it is because there is no light them" (KJV) In short, know your Bible, and know it well. Hide God's word deeply within your heart. Search the Scriptures daily and feed on the bread of life.

Then there are the words of Jesus about false prophets. He said, "You will recognize them by their fruits" (Matthew 7:16). We must hold the truth firmly, yet in love and humility. Our witness must be positive and winsome. Christ living through us should be plain and obvious. This way, we will not only reject the easy-going, pseudo-Christianity so popular today, but will be used of the Lord to help guide others away from these deadly paths of self-deception. Don't let a great leader's dying words be lost on you.

For Discussion and Reflection

1. How can we truly love the sinner and hate the sin? How can we steer clear of a quick judgmental attitude toward those who sin?

2. If sin is so spiritually dangerous, why do you suppose preachers, teachers, and congregations seem to avoid talking about it?

3. How might you identify a false teacher? What impact do false teachers have on individuals, church communities, and the wider community? Do you have personal experience with a false teacher? If so, how did his teaching bring the way of truth into disrepute? How do you avoid falling under the influence of a false prophet?

4. In 2 Peter 2:1, what do "destructive heresies" and "swift destruction" mean?

5. How was Lot affected by living in Sodom (Genesis 19)? How does the sinful world in which we live affect your life and your efforts to live in Christ?

7

The Return of Christ: Good News/Bad News

2 Peter 3:1-18

There are certain sentences, phrases, and words in the Bible which stand out like towering peaks of truth in the midst of a mighty mountain range of truth. Think of some of the grand and awesome words of Scripture:

> *In the beginning, God created ...[1] In the day you eat of it you shall surely die.[2] Noah found favor in the eyes of the Lord.[3] The Lord is my Shepherd ...[4] Fear not, I am with you ...[5] God so loved the world ...[6] I am the good Shepherd ...[7] Let not your hearts be troubled ...[8] By grace you have been saved through faith ...[9] The righteous shall live by faith ...[10] We know that for those who love God all things work together for good...[11]*

On and on we could go recalling great and wonderful words of Scripture, but don't leave out what may well be the grandest and most blessed of all: "The day of the Lord will come …"

Since there are over three hundred biblical references to the second coming of Christ, it amazes me that this great theme is seldom mentioned from most pulpits. We have allowed the often sensational and even weird interpretations of this grand event which flood the screens and the airways to deter us from a solid biblical and reformed interpretation, exposition, and proclamation of our one great hope and expectation. Shame on us!

These words written from death row, from a dying man to people facing death, sum up much of the teaching of the apostles, of Christ Himself, and indeed of the whole Bible. For believers, they are words of promise and hope. They make the Lord's Supper a feast of glorious anticipation. They carry us through the trials and tribulations of life, and they are like the first faint hints of light in the pre-dawn hours of the approaching day.

BUT these words are also the sound of approaching doom for those who do not belong to Christ. They are a sentence of death and destruction to this present world as we know it. They should strike terror in the hearts of the unbelieving and an awakening trumpet call to careless and indifferent Christians. These words should be like the angels who came to warn Lot of the impending fire storm awaiting Sodom and Gomorrah. When he delayed, they seized him by the hand to hurry him out of the doomed city. So may the Holy Spirit seize our hearts today, and save us from our bondage to this world.

I. The Certainty of that Day

Of all the many things which Christians should know about their Lord's return, the one most important truth above all is simply this: "The day of the Lord will come …" Have you ever read the essay C.S. Lewis wrote, "The World's Last Night"? Lewis said some very interesting and even thrilling things in that essay, but what gives it such power is his often-repeated sentence all through the essay, "There really will be a last night for the earth." This is expressed in different ways in various places in the Bible. Matthew 24:30: "They will see the Son of Man coming on the clouds of heaven with power and great glory." Acts 1:11: "This Jesus…will come in the same way as you saw him go into heaven." 1 Thessalonians 5:2: "The day of the Lord will come like a thief in the night." These are but a few of the positive assertions that our Lord is coming again in power, glory, and judgment. Let the scoffers scoff and the mockers mock, but the Day of the Lord will come!

Yes, we may and should enjoy this life to the fullest according to God's revealed pattern of godly living. We may and should provide for our families and live as good law-abiding citizens in an increasingly lawless world. We may and should build our new homes and church buildings, worship and serve the Lord in our short earthly life. BUT we should never forget that "The day of the Lord will come" and always be prepared for His return.

Though most people mock and scoff at the idea of a day of final judgment and laugh at Christians who believe that Christ will come again, when he comes in power and glory they will call on the rocks and mountains to fall on them to hide them from the wrath of the Lamb. There is no hiding place from that inevitable reckoning. No ocean deep enough, no mountain high enough, no island remote enough to hide from God in that day. "The day of the Lord will come." That is the great and glorious, and, yes, the awful and inescapable fact of the future.

II. The Terror of that Day

All biblical descriptions of that day are in terms of unbelievable and fearful devastation. It is impossible to talk about in such a way as to minimize the destruction or the terror of it. There have been many catastrophes of various kinds in the long history of this world, but put them all together, and they cannot compare in scope or intensity to "The Day of the Lord." First of all, it will be the ultimate surprise. There are several passages using almost identical language by saying, "It will come as a thief in the night." That implies that it is unexpected and that people will be unprepared. Some of you know what it is like to have your homes burglarized. You know it could happen, but you never expect it, and the sense of shock is profound and depressing beyond words.

All of us as Christians know in theory that the day of judgment will come upon this earth, but it is really beyond our imagination to try to think what it will be like. The end will be sudden and unexpected right up to the moment of His return. Jesus described this in Matthew 24:

> *For as in those days before the flood they were eating and drinking, marrying and giving in marriage, until the day when Noah entered the ark, and they were unaware until the flood came and swept them all away, so will be the coming of the Son of Man... Therefore, stay awake, for you do not know on what day your Lord is coming.*

There is another side to this. Both Jesus and the apostle Paul insisted that believers are not in the dark about the Lord's return. Certainly, we don't know the exact day or hour, but we are exhorted to be watchful. "You are not in darkness...for that day to surprise you like a thief," wrote Paul to the Thessalonians.

But it will not only be unexpected; it will be a catastrophe unprecedented. Hear these profound words once more. "The heavens will pass away with a roar, and the heavenly bodies will be burned up and dissolved, and the earth and the works that are done on it will be exposed...the heavens will be set on fire and dissolved, and the heavenly bodies will melt as they burn." Those are incredible words. They were written almost two thousand years ago, yet they sound like some of the modern scientific descriptions of how the world will one day end. Peter is echoing Jesus' words about this same end event. "The sun will be darkened, and the moon shall not give its light, the stars will fall from heaven, and the powers of the heavens will be shaken. Then...they will see the Son of Man coming on the clouds with power and great glory" (Matthew 24:29-30). By these words and many other similar words, we have to know that all natural or man-made catastrophes which have ever occurred in the long history of this planet will pale into insignificance.

We have read or heard of many mighty earthquakes in which thousands have died. We remember the scenes vividly portrayed on our TV screens of the unbelievable destruction caused by hurricanes, floods, and tornados just in recent years. We looked in shocked disbelief at the pictures of the Mount St. Helens eruption. The geological evidences of meteorites crashing into the earth are stunning in what they reveal.

We think, too, of such shocking events as the atom bomb blasts which brought World War II to its conclusion. Who can forget the shock and terror of actually seeing the airplanes plunging into the World Trade Center towers? Yet all these events, terrible and frightening as they are, cannot compare to the universal horror of what Peter describes in this passage.

Other Scriptures fill in a few of the details of which we need to be aware. All worldly government, systems, organizations, and works of any kind will come to a final and abrupt end. All the impressive and mighty works of man's ingenuity and labor will be destroyed. All commerce, trade, and financial empires will fall. There will be a sorting out of true believers from all others, including those who claim to know Christ and do not. There will be perfect, complete, and final separation and judgment.

III. The Day of the Lord for Believers

What a difference! Jesus said, "Now when these things begin to happen, look up and lift up your heads, because your redemption draws near" (Luke 21:28, NKJV). Peter said, "But according to His promise we are waiting for new heavens and a new earth in which righteousness dwells." Will the day of the Lord be fearful and dreadful beyond human imagination? Yes, and even more, but for believers it will be the fulfillment of all we hope and pray for. "The kingdom of the world has become the kingdom of our Lord and of his Christ, and he shall reign forever and ever" (Revelation 11:15). One day, we will no longer pray, "Thy Kingdom come, Thy will be done," for that prayer will have been answered. One day, we will no longer pray, "Forgive us our debts as we forgive our debtors," for all our sins will be revealed as forgiven and removed from God's sight and our minds forever. No longer will we have to struggle and battle against sin in our own hearts, or the consequences of sins against us by others. One day, we will no longer pray, "Lead us not into temptation, but deliver us from evil," for there will no longer be temptations to face, or evils with which to cope. But we will forever and ever pray and praise with these words: "For Thine is the kingdom, the power, and the glory forever," for this will be the glorious reality in which we will live for all eternity.

    The apostle Paul spoke of all creation being liberated from the bondage of death and decay when the Lord returns. The Old Testament prophets describe the renewed nature of the new creation, telling us that there will be no predator nor prey in this blissful future. The book of Revelation describes the beauty and glory of the new heavens and new earth in words that create a powerful longing for that day when there will be no more pain, sorrow, death, nor tears. Recently, in talking with a very dear brother who was terminally ill of cancer, and is now with the Lord, he said all he had to look forward to in this world was the next shot of pain killer, and he longed to be released. Truly, if in this world only we have hope, we are of all people the most to be pitied.

    "But, according to His promise, we are waiting for new heavens and a new earth in which righteousness dwells." So with eager faith and excited joy we are "waiting for and hastening the coming of the day of God." Yes, the day of the Lord as described in this passage from death row is fearful and awesome beyond anything we may imagine, but after the storm of judgment, we see a glimpse of the new heavens and the new earth in these words from Revelation 22:

7. THE RETURN OF CHRIST: GOOD NEWS/BAD NEWS

Then the angel showed me the river of the water of life, bright as crystal, flowing from the throne of God and of the Lamb through the middle of the street of the city; also, on either side of the river, the tree of life with its twelve kinds of fruit, yielding its fruit each month. The leaves of the tree were for the healing of the nations. No longer will there be anything accursed, but the throne of God and of the Lamb will be in it, and his servants will worship him. They will see his face, and his name will be on their foreheads. And night will be no more. They will need no light of lamp or sun, for the Lord God will be their light, and they will reign forever and ever.

When we come to the table of the Lord and celebrate Communion, we are reminded of our hope. Jesus promised that He would eat this bread and drink this cup new with us in the Father's kingdom. Here is our down payment, our token of hope until the fulfillment of all things. Soon the symbol will give way to the grand reality, the hope and promise to glorious and joyful completion. Jesus said, "Look up...because your redemption draws near." For the Day of the Lord will come!!!!! Hallelujah!!!!!!!!!!!!!!

For Discussion and Reflection

1. According 2 Peter 3, why is God delaying final judgment? What does the answer teach us about God?

2. Throughout Peter's letters, we are charged to "grow in the grace and knowledge of our Lord and Savior Jesus Christ" (2 Peter 3:18). In light of the preceding discussion and reflection upon 2 Peter 3, how can you go about this charge?

3. In this passage, Peter also charges us to get His message of salvation out to others (2 Peter 3:15). How can you address this charge in your daily life?

4. Peter begins this chapter of his second letter by restating that he is "stirring up your sincere mind by way of reminder." Why are reminders so important for Christians? How do you remind yourself of God's promises? How do you remind others?

5. Why does our culture resist the ideas of sin and repentance? Can there be salvation without repentance? Can you think of a time in your own life when repentance was difficult for you? Why was it difficult?

[1] Genesis 1:1
[2] Genesis 2:17
[3] Genesis 6:8
[4] Psalm 23:1
[5] Isaiah 41:10
[6] John 3:16
[7] John 10:11
[8] John 14:1
[9] Ephesians 2:8
[10] Romans 1:17
[11] Romans 8:28

8

THE RETURN OF CHRIST: THE SCOFFERS

2 Peter 3:1-18

What last words would you want to write to your loved ones just before your death? Peter's last words were words of hope and encouragement in the midst of dark and discouraging circumstances. Perhaps he was remembering that last sad but glorious moment with the Lord Jesus when He was taken away from Peter and the other disciples, ascending into heaven while they watched in gazing wonder. If that was what he was remembering as he sat in his cell awaiting execution, then surely Peter would have also remembered the promise the angel spoke when he said, "This same Jesus which you see taken up from you into heaven will come again in like manner as you have seen Him leave." How those words had lifted him up, driving away his sorrow and sustaining him as he joined with others in proclaiming the Gospel on the day of Pentecost and for thirty-some more years. Even now on death row, they gave him courage and hope.

So much of the teachings of Jesus and the writings of the apostles deal with the great theme of the return of the Lord. Go back even further to the Old Testament prophets and almost all of their prophecies of the coming of the Messiah had to do with both the first and second coming. Often, this was seen as one grand event. Many of the hymns we sing at Christmas about the birth of our Lord also include His return in glory. Too bad we sing them only at Christmastime.

In fact, Jesus based the validity of all His claims on His promised return in glory by which the unbelieving world will be judged, and the redeemed resurrected to an eternal kingdom of perfection and joy. Is there anything in the life and character of Jesus to suggest that He lied about this? Paul added his arguments for the resurrection and eternal life in 1 Corinthians 15 by saying, "If in this life only we have hope in Christ, we are of all men the most pitiable."

So when dying Peter reminded believers of the great and blessed hope of Christ's return in glory and judgment, he knew that it was precisely at this one point of true hope that unbelievers would concentrate their scorn and mocking. What was true in his day is even more so in ours. But take heart; it is the very presence and overwhelming numbers of these modern scorners that help prove the reliability of Scripture.

I. Who are these scoffers, and what are their arguments against Christ's return and against the Lord Himself?

Before answering that question, let me remind you this letter was written almost 2,000 years ago, but what is said here applies just as much to the twenty-first century as it does to the first. This alone tells us the Bible demands serious consideration. Peter makes some statements about the end times that can only be explained by special revelation from God. No first century man could have written these things based on human knowledge alone.

But the scoffers' reaction is summed up in these words: "Where is the promise of His coming? For ever since the fathers fell asleep, all things are continuing as they were from the beginning of creation." By these words of doubt, they attempt to destroy the whole case for Christianity. Their scoffing and mocking unbelief is based on two premises. (1) It has been a long time since He promised to return, and He still hasn't come back yet. Why should we believe in such fantastic stories? (2) Matter is eternal, and everything can be explained by a long-drawn-out process of evolution. Peter answers the last objection first because it is the more serious of the two.

Do you realize that the arguments of modern science in behalf of evolution grew out of a need to give scientific backing for a philosophy of atheism? A philosophy of unbelief developed in the continental universities during the so-called Age of "Enlightenment" well over two hundred years ago. This preceded any theory of evolution and was the philosophical foundation for the development of modern scientism. If there was no Creator, and if matter is eternal, and if things just developed on their own, this would require interminable eons of time. This is called uniformitarianism. The theories of the origin and development of the universe, and especially life and especially human life, did not grow out of a neutral vacuum of scientific enquiry, but rather grew out of the need to support a whole new concept of reality which left God completely out of the picture in any real sense.

All of this is presented as established fact, and those in the scientific community who point out the glaring inconsistencies and contradictions of evolution are the objects of persecution that is just as intolerant as the most brutal medieval inquisition. Many men of science are raising more and more questions about the assumptions and the so-called findings of the modern scoffers of Christ. Not all of these scholars are Christians, or even Theists. But they are screened out, discriminated against, ridiculed, and denied access to academia and to popular publications.

II. The Biblical answer to scoffers then and now

Peter accused these scoffers of old of the worst sort of sin: willful ignorance. What a charge to bring against learned men of science! But a person who willfully ignores contrary evidence to their own pet ideas is an ignorant person no matter what their degree of learning and, education.

8. THE RETURN OF CHRIST: THE SCOFFERS

Peter introduces two sharp criticisms of their position. First, the evidence of the past does not support their notions of atheism. Two grand events are introduced - Creation and the Flood. He rightly links the two together, for they were obviously acts of God and by the Word of God. To go beyond these fundamentals, the geological history of the world is overwhelmingly in favor of an ongoing series of catastrophic events: vast earthquakes, volcanic activity, meteorite activity, to name but a few categories. All these things fit right in to the biblical accounts of historical events which are noted in Scripture.

The point Peter makes is that the final catastrophe of a world-ending explosion and fire is consistent both with history as well as with the character of God. We are surrounded by a created universe that has the potential for the destruction of this world at any time. For instance, we live on a relatively thin crust of earth that floats on a molten mass of fire. When God calls for the last day, His mighty hand is filled with all the ammunition He needs to accomplish His will.

Lately, even those who hold so tenaciously to their discredited theories of uniformitarianism are beginning to concede the inevitability of a final judgment by fire, but they still don't want to see God's hand in this end. Furthermore, the Lord has demonstrated both His power and His will to judge the world and bring it to total destruction, and Peter reminds them and us of two past events to prove his point: the worldwide flood that destroyed ancient civilizations, and the gruesomely spectacular end of Sodom and Gomorrah.

The other scoffing objection Peter meets with similar undeniable logic is the matter of time. If God hasn't already done it, what is He waiting for? If Christ hasn't already returned, why should we believe He ever will? Time, said Peter, is one thing for mankind but another thing for God.

Several years ago, I visited with my two sisters. At that time, my oldest sister was still living. None of us had any idea what a short time on earth she had left to her. We had not seen each other very much or very often since our parents died. My older sister said something like this: "Here we are visiting just as if we saw each other every day because when we're together, it's just as if there has been no time passed since the last time."

Even for us, when we see friends and loved ones after many years of separation, it's just as if that time never was. So when we hear Peter saying, "With the Lord one day is as a thousand years, and a thousand years as one day," we can at least begin to understand what he meant. Time, we now know, is relative, and what seems like a long delay to man is not long to the eternal God. To God, the issues of this day are permanent and endless, and what happened a thousand years ago is present and real to Him. So, men are poor judges of time and its meaning.

But there is a far more profound reason for the apparent delay in the Lord's return. The other reason is the Lord's mercy and His kindness

8. THE RETURN OF CHRIST: THE SCOFFERS

towards wayward mankind. Listen to these words of Peter: "The Lord is not slow to fulfill His promise as some count slowness, but is patient toward you, not wising that any should perish but that all should reach repentance." Jesus said that at the end of the world, God will send forth His holy angels to gather the elect from every corner of the world. Not one person for whom the Lord Jesus died will ever be eternally lost. Until that complete number is gathered in, the Lord delays the Day of Judgment.

Why hasn't Jesus come back yet? God has yet to save all those for whom Christ died. But when that number is complete, He will not delay even for one more second. If you are reading or hearing these words, and you have never responded to God's amazing grace, you may be that one person God is waiting for to complete His gracious purpose.

Listen to the Spirit and the Word. The Lord is coming again to judge the living and the dead. "The day of the Lord will come ..." Don't be misled by high sounding criticism of God's Word. Don't let the mockers and scoffers lead you astray. Be watchful and be ready, for the Day of the Lord will come when you will meet Him. Will it be in mercy or in terrible judgment? Right now, the door of His mercy is open wide. He offers you forgiveness and grace. His Word proclaims the glorious news of salvation, that Christ Jesus died for sinners. That by His death on the cross, His resurrection from the dead, and His ascension into heaven, God has provided the perfect answer to your sins, your doubts and fears. This moment in time, God offers a glorious eternity for those who will repent and believe the Gospel. Will you now open your heart, repent, and receive His grace? For He will return soon, maybe very soon.

8. THE RETURN OF CHRIST: THE SCOFFERS

For Discussion and Reflection

1. Many passages in the Bible speak of the Lord's patience. In the case of 2 Peter, what does Peter give as the reason for His patience? Can you recall instances in which you personally benefited from God's patience? When and how?

2. It is difficult to bear up under scoffing and mockery. How do you guard against discouragement when someone mocks you? How do you respond when your faith is scorned?

3. Peter tells us that the Lord is delaying his Second Coming out of patience towards us, desiring that all of us come to repentance. Peter urges us to use this delay to grow in the grace and knowledge of our Lord, and to guard against being led astray. What might you do to strengthen your steadfastness, and to be more constant in your awareness of living as a child of God while awaiting the Father's return?

4. What did Paul mean when he wrote, "If in this life only we have hope in Christ, we are of all men the most pitiable."? (1 Corinthians 15:19)

5. As discussed in this chapter, many Christmas carols address the Second Coming. "Joy to the World" is based on Psalm 98, which proclaims the coming of the Kingdom of the Lord. Study Psalm 98 and "Joy to the World" in light of 2 Peter 3. Make note of the connections that you find among the three texts.

MOTIVATION FOR HOLY LIVING

2 Peter 3:10-18

They folded the letter, careful not to mar the writing or tear the fragile parchment. There was a sense of sadness mingled with awe. What they held in their hands was precious and sacred. Peter was now dead, and these were his last words...but more, they were the words of the Holy Spirit. They must be preserved at all cost and hidden from the unholy eyes of those who would destroy this precious legacy, even as they killed the apostle. Copies were made, some of which would be lost or destroyed in one way or another, but the Holy Spirit, who had rested on Peter as he wrote, would now make sure by His singular providence that these words would never be lost, for they were and are a part of the Word of God!

Now we, too, come to the end of this exciting and precious letter. Peter's last thoughts had been about the Lord's return in power and glory and the awful end of the ungodly. But his real purpose in reminding believers of this great truth was to stir up their minds and challenge them and us to consider what manner of persons we ought to be in view of the world's end, and the beginning of the new heaven and new earth God has prepared for us. Here we discover anew words which tell us what it means to live a life that honors God, and at the same time strengthen our assurance of salvation.

I can't tell you how important this is. Most of us sort of float along, confident of our relationship to the Lord and avoiding any serious soul-searching. Then, old age overtakes us, cancer is diagnosed, business or crops fail, our life-long mates are suddenly taken, and then we are faced with deep doubts and soul-searing fears. Or, as the Lord so graphically put it, "The rain fell, and the floods came..." (Matthew 7:25). Is the house built on rock or sand? Will it stand or fall?

When people really believe that the Lord is coming back again, they strive to build on the rock, knowing a life built on the shifting sands of this world will no more stand in the day of judgment than a house built on sand could withstand hurricane or flood. So, what does Peter tell us about preparing for our Lord's inevitable return?

I. Confidence in the Lord's return creates great hope in the believer.

The Bible seldom, if ever, uses the word 'hope' in the way we use it. When we talk of hope, it usually leaves a lot of room for disappointment and failure. We say things like, "I hope this illness soon passes"; "I hope it rains soon"; "I hope my kids turn out okay" (I'm never quite sure what 'okay' is). But when God speaks to us about hope, He is talking about a confident expectation of the fulfillment of His promises. Believers may hope "things will get better" in their present situation, having no real assurance they will get better. But when believers hope for the Lord's return and for a new heaven and a new earth, they express confidence that God will indeed do what He has promised. The really big issues of salvation by grace, the forgiveness of our sins, and assurance of God's love have already been settled, so we may truly live in hope that the Lord will return, and that God will restore His beautiful creation and make all things new.

We sing in the hymn *Rejoice, the Lord is King*, "Rejoice in glorious hope, the Lord our God shall come and take His servants up to their eternal home!" This glorious hope is anticipation of what will most surely come to pass: the return of our Lord Jesus Christ.

People who live in this hope are people who know how to live and how to die. They are people who can accept delay and disappointment. They are people who want their lives to count for God and who live to hear Him say one day, "Well done good and faithful servant." Go back for a moment and try to remember what Jesus taught about the final judgment as recorded in Matthew 25. What were the crucial issues in that scene? Jesus rewarded the elect on the basis of their faithfully carrying on His work by loving concern for the poor, helpless, and hurting masses. Saved by grace? Of course! But their works testified to the reality of their union with Christ. He also confronted the lost by pointing out they had failed to follow His example and show meaningful compassion, so their words of professed faith were empty and meaningless. Combine this with the words of Jesus to His disciples in the upper room as recorded in the Gospel of John: "Whoever believes in me will also do the works that I do" (John 14:12). How very crucial it is for believers to accept that challenge and responsibility. This is how we demonstrate that we are Christ's Church, by loving one another and becoming fishers of men.

II. Hope in the Lord's return inspires living at peace and being blameless in His sight.

Do you know what it is to live in peace? First of all, it implies a trusting peace towards God. When the Word tells us that the present world is going to be dissolved in fire, this is not a cause for panic; but rather we see this as an important link in the chain of redemption and glory. God has forgiven our sins and has given us His Holy Spirit as our Comforter and Guide. God has made peace with us! He has reconciled us to Himself.

Living in peace also means that we are at peace with our own consciences. The apostle Paul spoke about having the testimony of a good conscience before the Lord. This is not presumption; it is taking God at His word and accepting His wonderful amazing grace that we have been forgiven and adopted as His own precious children. This is the foundation for peace. If we look too much at ourselves, even with the good motive of wanting to examine ourselves before the Lord, we will give in to despair. As the old Scottish minister testified, "I looked into my own heart and found naught but blackness of sin. I looked to the Lord Jesus and saw naught but grace. 'Tis good we met."

But how do you reconcile the exhortation to live in peace, and at the same time the call to be blameless when we know our sinful nature? It just doesn't compute; or does it?

First of all, the call to be perfectly blameless is in one sense a goal towards which we are all striving, and never attaining in this life. On the other hand, believers are to avoid consciously giving offense to God or to man in so far as possible. This is not so much a call to sinless perfection of which none are capable, but to a life of integrity, humility, and love that does not bring dishonor on Christ. There simply must be a marked difference between the conduct of Christians and that of unbelievers.

The Bible describes Noah as a just and upright man who obviously walked with God. We know from the whole story that Noah was not a sinless man by any measure, but he was a man who obeyed God and tried to live his faith out before the world. Even after the great deliverance, he still had his old sin nature and his conduct, as described in Genesis 9:20, was far from blameless, to say the least.

The Bible calls David "a man after God's own heart," and he was. But was he sinless? No! Did he always live up to God's requirements? Again, the answer is no. But even at his worst, David always turned to God and found forgiveness and abounding grace. David broke many of his promises to God, but God never broke even one of His many great promises to David. Nor will he ever break His promises to you, for whom Christ died. He will never leave you or forsake you.

The big question is this: Can people look at your life and conduct and have a legitimate reason for rejecting Christ and His Church? Put it another way. Is there anything seen in you that would make people want to know the Savior whom you profess? That's what Peter meant when he called on believers to be "without spot and blameless."

III. Faith in Christ's return makes us steadfast.

Why do you think there are some Christians you can always count on? They are in church almost every time the doors are open. If any opportunity to give to the Lord's work is presented, they are the first to give. When Monday rolls around, they are the same kind of folks they were on Sunday. They respond to calls for prayer quickly and fervently. Why? Because they know the Lord is coming back again and they are ready at a moment's notice to welcome and greet Him. For them, the Lord's return is not so much a doctrine as it is an earnest expectation. They stand on the solid rock, they are not moved. I know there are not many like that, but all should be. Are you?

IV. Faith in Christ's return creates a desire to grow in grace and knowledge of our Lord.

Growing in grace and knowledge simply means an ever-deepening relationship with the Lord, and a living, growing relationship with Him and likeness to Him. Do you realize that's what salvation is all about? By grace you are saved through faith. It is a gift from God. But grace is not just a once and for all experience; it is a way of life that changes and transforms you into Christ-likeness. As some have put it: "You have been saved (Justification); you are being saved (Sanctification); you will be saved (Glorification)."

I remember when I was a little boy, if someone came calling at our house, my mother would always pause before she went to the door, take off her apron, quickly straighten her hair, and then open the door with a smile on her beautiful face. I think when all is said and done, that's what Simon Peter had in mind when he quickly wrote this little letter, just before he went home to be with the Lord.

You know what? Because of the work of grace in Peter's life, when he met Jesus in heaven, they had far more in common than just nail prints in their hands. Simon, who was sifted like wheat by the guiles of Satan, had at last become Peter the Rock, just like Jesus predicted. Now hear this, all you discouraged and doubtful Christians. You will be made perfect in holiness. You will be everything

God's Word calls on you to be. He who has begun a good work in you will perfect it in the day of Christ. So rejoice in glorious hope! Join the throngs who hailed Him as He entered the Holy City and cast palm branches before Him…only let your palm branches be faith and love.

9. MOTIVATION FOR HOLY LIVING

For Discussion and Reflection

1. Reflect upon your answer to the "big question": Can people look at your life and conduct and have a legitimate reason for rejecting Christ and His Church? Is there anything seen in you that would make people want to know the Savior whom you profess?

2. In this chapter, we considered faith and works. How do you demonstrate that you are a member of Christ's Church?

3. We reflected on the fact that there are a few in every congregation who stand solidly on their faith, ready at all times to meet the Lord whenever He comes. Are you one such Christian?

4. What does it mean to be blameless and spotless? How are you doing in those areas?

5. Are you ready for the Lord's return? Is your house built on rock or sand?